quick and easy
barbecue
meals

Styling DONNA HAY
Photography QUENTIN BACON

TRIDENT
PRESS
INTERNATIONAL

Introduction

There was a time when barbecuing was time consuming, tedious and not very elegant - not so today. The recipes, hints and tips in this book show that barbecuing can be more than charred steaks and sausages.

The wonderful array of dishes include Whole Fish in Banana Leaves, Thai Lamb and Noodle Salad and Festive Smoked Turkey just to name a few.

Owners of kettle or covered barbecues will find the chapter Undercover Cooking particularly useful - here there is a collection of recipes that make the most of this amazing piece of equipment, they include Slow-roasted Leg of Lamb with Barbecued Vegetables, Home-smoked Trout and Mango Berry Pudding.

Published by:
TRIDENT PRESS INTERNATIONAL
801 12th Avenue South
Suite 302
Naples, FL 34102 U.S.A.
(c)Trident Press
Tel: (941) 649 7077
Fax: (941) 649 5832
Email: tridentpress@worldnet.att.net
Website: www.trident-international.com

Quick & Easy Barbecue Meals

EDITORIAL
Food Editor: Rachel Blackmore
Editor: Linda Venturoni
Editorial and Production Assistant: Katrina O'Brien
Editorial Coordinator: Margaret Kelly
Food Stylist's Assistants and Recipe Development: Myles Beaufort, Jody Vassallo

Photography: Quentin Bacon
Styling: Donna Hay

DESIGN AND PRODUCTION
Manager: Anna Maguire
Picture Editor: Kirsten Holmes
Production Editor: Sheridan Packer
Trainee Production Editor: Danielle Thiris
Layout and Design: Lulu Dougherty
Cover Design: Michele Withers

Includes Index
ISBN 1 58279 346 8
EAN 9 781582 793467

First Edition Printed August 2001

Printed by Toppan Printing, China

ABOUT THIS BOOK

INGREDIENTS
Unless otherwise stated the following ingredients are used in this book:
Cream   Double, suitable for whipping
Flour   White flour, plain or standard
Sugar   White sugar

WHAT'S IN A TABLESPOON?
AUSTRALIA
1 tablespoon = 20 mL or 4 teaspoons
NEW ZEALAND
1 tablespoon = 15 mL or 3 teaspoons
UNITED KINGDOM
1 tablespoon = 15 mL or 3 teaspoons
The recipes in this book were tested in Australia where a 20 mL tablespoon is standard. The tablespoon in the New Zealand and the United Kingdom sets of measuring spoons is 15 mL. For recipes using baking powder, gelatine, bicarbonate of soda, small quantities of flour and cornflour, simply add another teaspoon for each tablespoon specified.

CANNED FOODS
Can sizes vary between countries and manufacturers. You may find the quantities in this book are slightly different to what is available. Purchase and use the can size nearest to the suggested size in the recipe.

HOW HOT?
In this book most of the recipes are cooked on a gas barbecue. If your barbecue uses coal, wood or barbecue fuel, you will need to allow 30-45 minutes for coals to heat and 45-60 minutes for wood. Most barbecuing is done over a medium fire - this is when the red glow will be almost gone and the ash becomes thicker and greyer in colour. When you hold your hand 15 cm/6 in above the coals you will be able to leave it there for 5-7 seconds.

CONTENTS

FINGER FOODS

Make the most of the barbecue and use it to prepare these tasty morsels. Serve one or two with drinks before a meal or present a selection to make a complete meal.

CHAR-GRILLED VEGETABLE SAMPLER

1 eggplant (aubergine), cut into
1 cm/^{1}/$_2$ in thick slices
salt
^{1}/$_3$ cup/90 mL/3 fl oz olive oil
6 plum (egg or Italian) tomatoes,
halved
6 spring onions, trimmed
1 teaspoon tarragon vinegar
1 yellow pepper, seeded and quartered
1 red pepper, seeded and quartered
2 zucchini (courgettes), cut lengthwise
into 5 mm/^{1}/$_4$ in thick slices
1 tablespoon balsamic vinegar
1 tablespoon honey
125 g/4 oz oyster mushrooms
1 teaspoon sesame oil
1 French bread stick, cut into
1 cm/^{1}/$_2$ in thick slices
1 clove garlic, cut in half

Accompany with a
selection of your favourite
dipping sauces, such as
tahini, pesto and sweet
chilli sauce. For a simple
and delicious presentation
simply sprinkle with
balsamic vinegar and
chopped fresh herbs of
your choice.

1 Preheat barbecue to a medium heat.
Place eggplant (aubergine) in a colander,
sprinkle with salt and set aside to drain
for 15 minutes. Rinse under cold water
and pat dry with absorbent kitchen
paper. Brush slices lightly with olive oil.

2 Combine the following in separate
bowls: tomatoes, spring onions, tarragon
vinegar and 1 tablespoon olive oil; yellow
pepper, red pepper, zucchini (courgettes),
balsamic vinegar and honey; mushrooms
and sesame oil and toss to combine. Rub
bread slices with cut surface of garlic and
lightly brush with olive oil.

3 Place eggplant (aubergine),
tomatoes, spring onions, yellow pepper,
red pepper, zucchini (courgettes)
mushrooms and bread slices on lightly
oiled barbecue grill and cook, turning
occasionally, for 5-10 minutes or until
vegetables are cooked. To serve,
arrange on a large serving platter.

Serves 6

MIDDLE EASTERN DIP

1 large eggplant (aubergine)
1 onion, unpeeled
2 cloves garlic, crushed
olive oil
2 tablespoons lemon juice
2 tablespoons chopped fresh parsley
^{1}/$_4$ cup/60 g/2 oz sour cream
4 pieces lavash bread, cut into triangles

Lavash bread is a yeast-
free Middle Eastern bread
available from Middle
Eastern food shops and
some supermarkets. If
unavailable use pitta bread
instead.

1 Preheat barbecue to a high heat.
Place eggplant (aubergine) and onion
on lightly oiled barbecue grill and cook,
turning occasionally, for 20-30 minutes
or until skins of eggplant (aubergine)
and onion are charred and flesh is soft.
Cool slightly, peel and chop roughly.

2 Place eggplant (aubergine), onion,
garlic, ^{1}/$_4$ cup/60 mL/2 fl oz oil and lemon
juice in a food processor or blender and
process until smooth. Add parsley and
sour cream and mix to combine.

3 Brush bread lightly with oil and cook
on barbecue for 1-2 minutes each side or
until crisp. Serve immediately with dip.

Serves 6

Cajun Chicken with Lime Sauce

CAJUN CHICKEN WITH LIME SAUCE

4 boneless chicken breast fillets, cut into 2 cm/^{3}/4 in wide strips

CAJUN SPICE MIX
5 cloves garlic, crushed
4 tablespoons paprika
2 tablespoons dried oregano
2 tablespoons dried thyme
2 teaspoons salt
2 teaspoons freshly ground black pepper

LIME DIPPING SAUCE
1^1/2 cups/315 g/10 oz low-fat natural yogurt
2 tablespoons fresh lime juice
1 tablespoon finely grated lime rind
1 teaspoon lime juice cordial

1   Preheat barbecue to a high heat.

2   To make spice mix, place garlic, paprika, oregano, thyme, salt and black pepper in a bowl and mix to combine. Add chicken and toss to coat. Shake off excess spice mix and cook, turning frequently, on lightly oiled barbecue plate (griddle) for 5-7 minutes or until chicken is tender.

3   To make sauce, place yogurt, lime juice, lime rind and cordial in a bowl and mix to combine. Serve with chicken.

Serves 6

For an attractive presentation, place a bowl of dipping sauce in the centre of a serving platter, surround with chicken and garnish with lime wedges.

CRANBERRY CHICKEN SKEWERS

750 g/1¹/₂ lb chicken mince
¹/₂ cup/30 g/1 oz breadcrumbs, made
from stale bread
1 onion, diced
2 cloves garlic, crushed
2 tablespoons chopped fresh sage or
1 teaspoon dried sage
1 teaspoon ground mixed spice
1 egg, lightly beaten
¹/₄ teaspoon Tabasco sauce or
according to taste
¹/₂ cup/125 mL/4 fl oz cranberry
sauce, warmed

1 Place chicken, breadcrumbs, onion, garlic, sage, mixed spice, egg and Tabasco sauce in a bowl and mix to combine.

2 Shape chicken mixture around lightly oiled skewers to form 7.5 cm/ 3 in sausage shapes. Place skewers on a plate, cover and refrigerate for 2 hours.

3 Preheat barbecue to a medium heat. Place skewers on lightly oiled barbecue grill and cook, turning several times, for 5-10 minutes or until skewers are cooked. Drizzle with cranberry sauce and serve immediately.

Serves 6

Remember always check the barbecue area before lighting the barbecue. Do not have the barbecue too close to the house and sweep up any dry leaves or anything that might catch fire if hit by a spark.

ORIENTAL CHICKEN LIVERS

125 g/4 oz chicken livers, trimmed,
cleaned and cut into sixteen pieces
8 water chestnuts, halved
8 rashers bacon, rind removed
and cut in half

ORIENTAL MARINADE
1 teaspoon brown sugar
1 tablespoon hot water
2 tablespoons soy sauce
1 tablespoon oyster sauce
¹/₂ teaspoon five spice powder
2 cloves garlic, crushed

1 To make marinade, place sugar and water in a bowl and mix to dissolve sugar. Add soy sauce, oyster sauce, five spice powder and garlic and mix to combine. Add chicken livers, cover and marinate in the refrigerator for 3 hours.

2 Preheat barbecue to a high heat. Drain livers well. Place a piece of liver and water chestnut on each piece of bacon and wrap to enclose. Secure with a wooden toothpick or cocktail stick. Place on lightly oiled barbecue grill and cook, turning several times, for 6-8 minutes or until bacon is crisp and livers are just cooked.

Makes 16

Heat the barbecue plate (griddle) or grill and brush lightly with oil before adding the food. This will prevent the food sticking to the barbecue. Remember when brushing with oil to use a brush that can withstand heat – if you use one with nylon bristles they will melt.

Cranberry Chicken Skewers,
Oriental Chicken Livers

Mushroom Risotto Cakes

30 g/1 oz butter
1 tablespoon olive oil
2 cloves garlic, crushed
3 rashers bacon, chopped
1 leek, thinly sliced
1¼ cups/280 g/9 oz Arborio or risotto rice
125 g/4 oz button mushrooms, sliced
3 cups/750 mL/1¼ pt hot chicken or vegetable stock
1 cup/250 mL/8 fl oz dry white wine
60 g/2 oz grated Parmesan cheese
freshly ground black pepper
¼ cup/30 g/1 oz flour
2 eggs, lightly beaten
1½ cups/90 g/3 oz wholemeal breadcrumbs, made from stale bread

These bite-sized morsels are sure to be a hit with drinks before any barbecue. They can also be cooked in a frying pan over a medium heat on the cooker top. For a vegetarian version of this recipe omit the bacon and use vegetable stock.

1   Melt butter and oil together in saucepan over a medium heat, add garlic and bacon and cook, stirring, for 3 minutes or until bacon is crisp. Add leek and cook for 3 minutes or until leek is golden. Add rice and mushrooms to pan and cook, stirring, for 3 minutes longer.

2   Stir in ¾ cup/185 mL/6 fl oz hot stock and ¼ cup/60 mL/2 fl oz wine and cook, stirring constantly, over a medium heat until liquid is absorbed. Continue adding stock and wine in this way, stirring constantly and allowing liquid to be absorbed before adding more.

3   Remove pan from heat, add Parmesan cheese and black pepper to taste and mix to combine. Set aside to cool, then refrigerate for at least 3 hours.

4   Preheat barbecue to a medium heat. Shape tablespoons of rice mixture into patties. Toss in flour to coat and shake off excess. Dip patties in eggs and roll in breadcrumbs to coat. Cook patties on lightly oiled barbecue plate (griddle) for 5 minutes each side or until golden and heated through.

Serves 6

Plates Villeroy & Boch

Mushroom Risotto Cakes

TANDOORI MIXED PLATTER

6 lamb cutlets, trimmed of excess fat
2 boneless chicken breast fillets
18 uncooked medium prawns, shelled
and deveined, tails left intact
250 g/8 oz rump steak, cut
into thin strips

TANDOORI MARINADE
2 tablespoons Tandoori seasoning
or paste
1 tablespoon ground coriander
$1^1/_2$ cups/315 g/10 oz low-fat
natural yogurt
1 tablespoon lemon juice

BANANA HERB YOGURT
1 banana, sliced
2 tablespoons chopped fresh mint
2 tablespoons desiccated coconut
1 cup/200 g/6$^1/_2$ oz low-fat
natural yogurt

1   To make marinade, place Tandoori seasoning or paste, coriander, yogurt and lemon juice in a bowl and mix to combine.

2   Place lamb cutlets and chicken in separate shallow glass or ceramic dishes, spoon one-quarter of marinade over each, toss to coat and cover. Thread prawns onto lightly oiled skewers and place on a plate. Thread beef onto lightly oiled skewers and place on a separate plate. Brush kebabs with remaining marinade and cover. Marinate lamb, chicken, prawns and beef in the refrigerator for 3 hours.

3   To make Banana Herb Yogurt, place banana, mint, coconut and yogurt in a bowl and mix to combine. Cover and refrigerate until required.

4   Preheat barbecue to a medium heat. Drain lamb, chicken, prawns and beef, place on lightly oiled barbecue grill and cook, turning several times, for 5-10 minutes or until all ingredients are cooked and tender.

5   To serve, cut chicken into 1 cm/$^1/_2$ in thick slices and arrange attractively on a large serving platter with lamb cutlets, prawn kebabs and beef kebabs. Serve with Banana Herb Yogurt.

Serves 6

Remember to soak bamboo or wooden skewers in water before using – this prevents them from burning during cooking. Before threading food onto skewers, lightly oil them so that the cooked food is easy to remove.

Tandoori Mixed Platter

Plate Villeroy & Boch

Spicy Barbecued Nuts

250 g/8 oz honey roasted peanuts
185 g/6 oz pecans
125 g/4 oz macadamia nuts
125 g/4 oz cashews
1 tablespoon sweet paprika
1 tablespoon ground cumin
2 teaspoons garam masala
1 teaspoon ground coriander
1 teaspoon ground nutmeg
$^{1}/_{4}$ teaspoon cayenne pepper or
according to taste
1 tablespoon olive oil

1 Preheat barbecue to a medium heat. Place peanuts, pecans, macadamia nuts and cashews in a bowl and mix to combine. Add paprika, cumin, garam masala, coriander, nutmeg and cayenne pepper and toss to coat.

2 Heat oil on barbecue plate (griddle), add nut mixture and cook, turning frequently, for 5 minutes or until nuts are golden. Cool slightly before serving.

Serves 6

Warning – the nuts are very hot when first removed from the barbecue and they retain their heat for quite a long time – so caution your guests when you serve these delicious nibbles.

Gingered Beef Sticks

500 g/1 lb rump steak, trimmed of all visible fat and cut into thin strips

GINGER MARINADE
2 spring onions, finely chopped
2 teaspoons finely grated fresh ginger
1 teaspoon crushed black peppercorns
$^{1}/_{4}$ cup/60 mL/2 fl oz Japanese soy sauce
2 tablespoons brown sugar
2 tablespoons sake or dry sherry (optional)

1 To make marinade, place spring onions, ginger, black peppercorns, soy sauce, sugar and sake or sherry, if using, in a bowl and mix to combine. Add beef, toss to coat and marinate for 1-2 hours at room temperature or overnight in the refrigerator.

2 Preheat barbecue to a medium heat. Drain beef and thread onto lightly oiled skewers. Cook skewers on barbecue for 1-2 minutes each side or until cooked to your liking.

Serves 4-6

Japanese soy sauce, also known as tamari and tamari shoyu, is available from Oriental food shops and some supermarkets. Like the better known Chinese soy sauce it is made from soya beans – it contains no added MSG (monosodium glutamate) but does contain significant amounts of naturally occurring sodium and MSG. If it is unavailable Chinese soy sauce can be used but the flavour will be slightly different.

Gingered Beef Sticks, Spicy Barbecued Nuts

SUCCULENT SEAFOOD

With their quick cooking times fish and seafood are perfect for barbecuing. This imaginative selection of dishes will have you serving these water creatures from the barbecue regularly.

Previous pages: Grilled Cod and Potatoes, Whole Fish in Banana Leaves
Plate Villeroy & Boch

WHOLE FISH IN BANANA LEAVES

1 large banana leaf
1 large whole fish such as bream, sea perch or snapper, cleaned and skin scored at 3 cm/1^1/4 in intervals
1 lime, thinly sliced
4 sprigs fresh dill

NUTTY RICE STUFFING
1 cup/220 g/7 oz wild rice blend, cooked
90 g/3 oz pistachio nuts, chopped
3 tablespoons finely chopped sun-dried peppers or tomatoes
3 spring onions, chopped
1 tablespoon chopped fresh dill
1 teaspoon finely grated lemon rind
1 clove garlic, chopped

Wild rice blend is a mix of wild rice and brown rice. If unavailable you can make your own by combining one part wild rice with two parts brown rice. As the cooking times of the two are similar they can be cooked together. Banana leaves can be purchased from Oriental food shops and some supermarkets.

1   Preheat barbecue to a medium heat. Blanch banana leaf in boiling water for 1 minute, drain, pat dry and set aside.

2   To make stuffing, place rice, pistachio nuts, sun-dried peppers or tomatoes, spring onions, dill, lemon rind and garlic in a bowl and mix to combine. Spoon stuffing into cavity of fish and secure opening with wooden toothpicks or cocktail sticks.

3   Place fish in centre of banana leaf, top with lime slices and dill and fold banana leaf around fish to completely enclose. Secure with wooden toothpicks or cocktail sticks. Alternately wrap fish in lightly oiled aluminium foil.

4   Place fish on barbecue grill and cook for 7-10 minutes, turn and cook for 7-10 minutes longer or until flesh flakes when tested with a fork.

Serves 4

GRILLED COD AND POTATOES

3 tablespoons olive oil
2 tablespoons lime juice
1 teaspoon crushed black peppercorns
4 cod cutlets
6 potatoes, very thinly sliced
sea salt

This tasty dish is delicious served with spicy tomato salsa or lime-flavoured mayonnaise. To make lime-flavoured mayonnaise, place ^{1}/4 cup/60 mL/2 fl oz mayonnaise, ^{1}/4 cup/45 g/1^1/2 oz natural yogurt, 1 tablespoon fresh lime juice and 1 teaspoon grated lime rind in a bowl and mix to combine.

1   Preheat barbecue to a medium heat. Place 1 tablespoon oil, lime juice and black peppercorns in a bowl and mix to combine. Brush oil mixture over fish and marinate at room temperature for 10 minutes.

2   Brush potatoes with oil and sprinkle with salt. Place potatoes on lightly oiled barbecue grill and cook for 5 minutes each side or until tender and golden. Move potatoes to side of barbecue to keep warm.

3   Place fish on lightly oiled barbecue grill and cook for 3-5 minutes each side or until flesh flakes when tested with a fork. To serve, arrange potatoes attractively on serving plates and top with fish.

Serves 4

SQUID AND SCALLOP SALAD

1 red pepper, seeded and halved
1 yellow or green pepper, seeded
and halved
2 squid (calamari) tubes
250 g/8 oz scallops, roe (coral) removed
250 g/8 oz asparagus, cut into
5 cm/2 in pieces, blanched
1 red onion, sliced
3 tablespoons fresh coriander leaves
1 bunch rocket or watercress

HERB AND BALSAMIC DRESSING
1 tablespoon finely grated fresh ginger
1 tablespoon chopped fresh rosemary
1 clove garlic, crushed
$^1/_4$ cup/60 mL/2 fl oz olive oil
2 tablespoons lime juice
1 tablespoon balsamic or
red wine vinegar

1   To make dressing, place ginger, rosemary, garlic, oil, lime juice and vinegar in a screwtop jar and shake well to combine. Set aside.

2   Preheat barbecue to a high heat. Place red and yellow or green pepper halves, skin side down on lightly oiled barbecue grill and cook for 5-10 minutes or until skins are blistered and charred. Place peppers in a plastic food bag or paper bag and set aside until cool enough to handle. Remove skins from peppers and cut flesh into thin strips.

3   Cut squid (calamari) tubes lengthwise and open out flat. Using a sharp knife cut parallel lines down the length of the squid (calamari), taking care not to cut through the flesh. Make more cuts in the opposite direction to form a diamond pattern. Cut into 5 cm/2 in squares.

4   Place squid (calamari) and scallops on lightly oiled barbecue plate (griddle) and cook, turning several times, for 3 minutes or until tender. Set aside to cool slightly.

5   Combine red and yellow or green peppers, asparagus, onion and coriander. Line a large serving platter with rocket or watercress, top with vegetables, squid (calamari) and scallops. Drizzle with dressing and serve immediately.

Serves 4

To blanch asparagus, boil, steam or microwave until it just changes colour. Drain well and refresh under cold running water.

Squid and Scallop Salad

Plate Villeroy & Boch

SALMON SKEWERS

500 g/1 lb salmon fillet, cut into
2.5 cm/1 in squares
250 g/8 oz snow peas (mangetout),
trimmed
1 tablespoon wholegrain mustard
2 teaspoons chopped fresh lemon
thyme or thyme
$^1/_2$ teaspoon ground cumin
2 tablespoons lemon juice
2 teaspoons honey

1   Preheat barbecue to a medium heat. Thread salmon and snow peas (mangetout), alternately, onto lightly oiled skewers.

2   Place mustard, thyme, cumin, lemon juice and honey in a bowl and mix to combine. Brush mustard mixture over salmon and cook on lightly oiled barbecue grill for 2-3 minutes each side or until salmon is just cooked.

Serves 4

Watch a lit barbecue at all times and keep children and pets away from hot barbecues and equipment.

TIKKA SKEWERS

750 g/1$^1/_2$ lb firm white fish fillets,
cut into 2 cm/$^3/_4$ in wide strips
1 lemon, cut into wedges

SPICY YOGURT MARINADE
1 onion, chopped
4 cloves garlic, crushed
2 teaspoons finely grated fresh ginger
1 tablespoon ground cumin
1 tablespoon garam masala
3 cardamom pods, crushed
1 teaspoon ground turmeric
2 teaspoons chilli powder
2 teaspoons ground coriander
1 tablespoon tomato paste (purée)
1$^3/_4$ cups/350 g/11 oz natural yogurt

CUCUMBER RAITHA
1 cucumber, finely chopped
1 tablespoon chopped fresh mint
1 cup/200 g/6$^1/_2$ oz natural yogurt

1   Pierce fish strips several times with a fork and place in a shallow glass or ceramic dish.

2   To make marinade, place onion, garlic, ginger, cumin, garam masala, cardamom, turmeric, chilli powder, coriander and tomato paste (purée) in a food processor or blender and process until smooth. Add yogurt and mix to combine. Spoon marinade over fish, toss to combine, cover and marinate in the refrigerator for 3 hours.

3   Preheat barbecue to a medium heat. Drain fish and thread onto lightly oiled skewers. Place skewers on lightly oiled barbecue grill and cook, turning several times, for 5-6 minutes or until fish is cooked.

4   To make raitha, place cucumber, mint and yogurt in a bowl and mix to combine. Serve skewers with lemon wedges and raitha.

Serves 6

When buying fish fillets look for those that are shiny and firm with a pleasant sea smell. Avoid those that are dull, soft, discoloured or oozing water when touched.

Blue plate Villeroy & Boch

Salmon Skewers, Tikka Skewers

BLACKENED TUNA STEAKS

4 thick tuna steaks
2 tablespoons olive oil

CAJUN SPICE MIX
2 tablespoons sweet paprika
1 tablespoon dried ground garlic
1 tablespoon onion powder
2 teaspoons crushed black
peppercorns
2 teaspoons dried mixed herbs
1 teaspoon cayenne pepper

FENNEL TOMATO SALSA
4 plum (egg or Italian tomatoes),
chopped
1 bulb fennel, finely chopped
1 red onion, finely chopped
2 tablespoons capers
1 tablespoon chopped fresh mint
1 clove garlic, crushed
1 tablespoon lemon juice
1 tablespoon orange juice

1   Preheat barbecue to a high heat.
To make salsa, place tomatoes, fennel,
onion, capers, mint, garlic, lemon juice
and orange juice in a bowl and toss to
combine. Set aside until ready to serve.

2   To make spice mix, place paprika,
ground garlic, onion powder, black
peppercorns, herbs and cayenne pepper
in a bowl and mix to combine. Add
tuna, toss to coat and shake off excess.

3   Heat oil on barbecue plate (griddle)
for 2-3 minutes or until hot, add tuna
and cook for 3-4 minutes each side or
until blackened and cooked to your
liking. Serve immediately with salsa.

Serves 4

If tuna is unavailable
swordfish or salmon are
delicious alternatives. Dried
ground garlic is available
in the spice section of
supermarkets. It has a
pungent taste and smell
and should be used with
care.

Left: Blackened Tuna Steaks
Above: Oysters and Mussels in Shells

OYSTERS AND MUSSELS IN SHELLS

500 g/1 lb mussels, scrubbed and
beards removed
24 oysters in half shells
60 g/2 oz butter, softened
1 tablespoon chopped fresh parsley
2 tablespoons lemon juice
1 tablespoon orange juice
1 tablespoon white wine

1   Preheat barbecue to a high heat.
Place mussels and oysters on barbecue
grill and cook for 3-5 minutes or until
mussel shells open and oysters are
warm. Discard any mussels that do not
open after 5 minutes cooking.

2   Place butter, parsley, lemon juice,
orange juice and wine in a heavy-based
saucepan, place on barbecue and cook,
stirring, for 2 minutes or until mixture
is bubbling. Place mussels and oysters
on a serving platter, drizzle with butter
mixture and serve immediately.

Serves 6

Mussels will live out of water
for up to 7 days if treated
correctly. To keep mussels
alive, place them in a
bucket, cover with a wet
towel and top with ice.
Store in a cool place and
as the ice melts, drain off
the water and replace ice.
It is important that the
mussels do not sit in the
water or they will drown.

LEMON GRASS PRAWNS

1 kg/2 lb uncooked medium prawns
3 stalks fresh lemon grass, finely
chopped
2 spring onions, chopped
2 small fresh red chillies, finely
chopped
2 cloves garlic, crushed
2 tablespoons finely grated
fresh ginger
1 teaspoon shrimp paste
1 tablespoon brown sugar
$^1/_2$ cup/125 mL/4 fl oz coconut milk

1 Wash prawns, leaving shells and heads intact and place in a shallow glass or ceramic dish.

2 Place lemon grass, spring onions, chillies, garlic, ginger and shrimp paste in a food processor or blender and process until smooth. Add sugar and coconut milk and process to combine. Spoon mixture over prawns, toss to combine, cover and marinate in the refrigerator for 3-4 hours.

3 Preheat barbecue to a high heat. Drain prawns, place on barbecue and cook, turning several times, for 5 minutes or until prawns change colour. Serve immediately.

Serves 4

Fresh lemon grass and shrimp paste are available from Oriental food shops and some supermarkets. Lemon grass can also be purchased dried; if using dried lemon grass, soak it in hot water for 20 minutes or until soft before using. It is also available in bottles from supermarkets, use this in the same way as you would fresh lemon grass.

SESAME PRAWN CAKES

315 g/10 oz uncooked, shelled and
deveined prawns
250 g/8 oz fresh crab meat
3 spring onions, chopped
2 tablespoons finely chopped
fresh basil
1 fresh red chilli, finely chopped
1 teaspoon ground cumin
1 teaspoon paprika
1 egg white
155 g/5 oz sesame seeds
1 tablespoon vegetable oil

1 Preheat barbecue to a medium heat. Place prawns, crab meat, spring onions, basil, chilli, cumin, paprika and egg white into a food processor and process until well combined. Take 4 tablespoons of mixture, shape into a pattie and roll in sesame seeds to coat. Repeat with remaining mixture to make six patties.

2 Heat oil on barbecue plate (griddle) for 2-3 minutes or until hot, add patties and cook for 10 minutes each side or until patties are golden and cooked.

Serves 6

If fresh crab meat is unavailable drained canned crab can be used instead. These fish cakes are delicious served with a sweet chilli sauce for dipping. Sweet chilli sauce is available from Oriental food shops and some supermarkets.

*Lemon Grass Prawns,
Sesame Prawn Cakes*

PERFECT POULTRY

This exciting selection of recipes for chicken, duck and quail are sure to become barbecue favourites. Included are such tempting dishes as Chicken Pesto Burgers, Plum Duck Salad and Indian Yogurt Kebabs.

GRILLED CHICKEN SALAD

2 tablespoons chopped fresh coriander
1 fresh red chilli, chopped
2 tablespoons soy sauce
2 tablespoons lime juice
4 boneless chicken breast fillets
1 bunch rocket or watercress
250 g/8 oz cherry tomatoes, halved
155 g/5 oz feta cheese, crumbled
90 g/3 oz marinated olives

LIME DRESSING
2 tablespoons olive oil
2 tablespoons lime juice
freshly ground black pepper

The chicken will come to no harm if marinated for longer than 30 minutes, but if you think the marinating will exceed 1 hour it is safer to place it in the refrigerator. When entertaining this recipe can be prepared to the end of step 3 several hours in advance, cover and store in the refrigerator until required.

1 Place coriander, chilli, soy sauce and lime juice in a bowl and mix to combine. Add chicken, toss to coat and marinate at room temperature for 30 minutes.

2 Preheat barbecue to a medium heat. Arrange rocket or watercress, tomatoes, feta cheese and olives attractively on a serving platter. Set aside.

3 To make dressing, place oil, lime juice and black pepper to taste in a screwtop jar and shake well to combine. Set aside.

4 Drain chicken, place on lightly oiled barbecue grill and cook for 4-5 minutes each side or until cooked through. Slice chicken, arrange on salad, drizzle with dressing and serve immediately.

Serves 4

SPICY MANGO CHICKEN

4 boneless chicken breast fillets
1 teaspoon freshly ground
black pepper
1 teaspoon ground cumin
1 teaspoon paprika
4 slices prosciutto or ham, halved
2 mangoes, peeled and cut
into 2 cm/³/4 in thick slices

MANGO SAUCE
1 mango, peeled and chopped
1 clove garlic, crushed
2 tablespoons golden syrup
1 tablespoon sweet chilli sauce

Drained, canned mangoes can be used in place of fresh. You will need two 440 g/14 oz cans of mangoes. Use three-quarters of one can for the sauce and the remainder for the filling in the chicken.

1 Preheat barbecue to a high heat. Place chicken between sheets of greaseproof paper and pound lightly with a meat mallet to flatten to 1 cm/¹/2 in thick.

2 Combine black pepper, cumin and paprika and sprinkle over chicken. Layer prosciutto or ham and mango slices on chicken, roll up and secure with wooden toothpicks or cocktail sticks. Place chicken on lightly oiled barbecue and cook for 3-5 minutes each side or until chicken is tender and cooked.

3 To make sauce, place mango, garlic, golden syrup and chilli sauce in a small saucepan and cook, stirring, over a low heat for 4-5 minutes or until sauce thickens slightly. Serve with chicken.

Serves 4

Fragrant Orange Quail

FRAGRANT ORANGE QUAIL

6 quail, halved

BRANDY ORANGE MARINADE
6 tablespoons chopped fresh
mixed herbs
2 tablespoons Dijon mustard
1 tablespoon finely grated orange rind
2 cloves garlic, crushed
$^1/_2$ cup/125 mL/4 fl oz cider
$^1/_2$ cup/125 mL/4 fl oz orange juice
$^1/_4$ cup/60 mL/2 fl oz brandy
1 tablespoon macadamia or walnut oil

NUTTY COUSCOUS
1 cup/185 g/6 oz couscous
2 cups/500 mL/16 fl oz boiling water
90 g/3 oz sultanas
60 g/2 oz hazelnuts, toasted and
chopped
2 spring onions, chopped
1 tablespoon lemon juice

Serves 4

1   To make marinade, place herbs, mustard, orange rind, garlic, cider, orange juice, brandy and oil in a shallow glass or ceramic dish and mix to combine. Add quail, turn to coat, cover and marinate in the refrigerator for 2 hours.

2   Preheat barbecue to a medium heat. Drain quail, place skin side up, on lightly oiled barbecue grill and cook, turning occasionally, for 10 minutes or until quail is tender.

3   For couscous, place couscous in a bowl, pour over boiling water, cover and set aside to stand for 10 minutes or until water is absorbed. Toss with a fork, add sultanas, hazelnuts, spring onions and lemon juice and toss to combine. To serve, line a large serving platter with couscous then arrange quail attractively on top.

Often thought of as a type of grain couscous is actually a pasta made from durum wheat, however cook and use it in the same way as a grain. The name couscous refers to both the raw product and the cooked dish. It is an excellent source of thiamin and iron as well as being a good source of protein and niacin.

Plates Villeroy & Boch

CHICKEN IN COALS

1.5 kg/3 lb chicken
60 g/2 oz butter, melted
2 tablespoons soy sauce
1 tablespoon honey
2 star anise
1 cinnamon stick

For this recipe the chicken is actually cooked in the coals of the barbecue so it is important that the fire is not too hot. If using wood the fire should burn down to red hot glowing embers. When using charcoal or heat beads the coals should be glowing and partially covered by grey ash. Charcoal takes 15-20 minutes to reach this stage, heat beads 30-40 minutes and wood an hour or more, depending on the variety used.

1 Heat barbecue until flames die down and coals are glowing. The barbecue is ready when you can hold your hand about 10 cm/4 in from the coals for 4-5 seconds.

2 Cut chicken down back bone and press to flatten. Place butter, soy sauce and honey in a bowl and mix to combine. Brush butter mixture over chicken and place on a sheet of nonstick baking paper large enough to completely enclose chicken. Top chicken with star anise and cinnamon stick and wrap in baking paper. Then wrap paper parcel in a double thickness of aluminium foil.

3 Place chicken in coals and cook, turning several times, for 45-60 minutes or until chicken is cooked and tender.

Serves 4

INDIAN YOGURT KEBABS

6 chicken thigh fillets, halved

YOGURT MARINADE
1 tablespoon chopped fresh coriander
2 teaspoons finely grated fresh ginger
1 clove garlic, crushed
2 teaspoons paprika
1 teaspoon ground cumin
$^1/_2$ teaspoon ground turmeric
$^1/_2$ teaspoon chilli powder
$^1/_2$ teaspoon ground cinnamon
1 cup/200 g/6$^1/_2$ oz natural yogurt
2 tablespoons lemon juice

If chicken thigh fillets are unavailable chicken breast fillets can be used instead. You will need 3 boneless chicken breast fillets, each cut into four pieces.

1 To make marinade, place coriander, ginger, garlic, paprika, cumin, turmeric, chilli powder, cinnamon, yogurt and lemon juice in a shallow glass or ceramic dish and mix well to combine. Add chicken, toss to coat and marinate at room temperature for 30 minutes.

2 Preheat barbecue to a medium heat. Drain chicken and thread three pieces onto a lightly oiled skewer. Repeat with remaining chicken to make four kebabs. Place kebabs on lightly oiled barbecue grill and cook for 4-5 minutes each side or until chicken is cooked and tender.

Serves 4

Chicken in Coals, Indian Yogurt Kebabs

PLUM DUCK SALAD

3 duck breasts, skinned
2 onions, thinly sliced
1 mizuna lettuce, leaves separated
185 g/6 oz snow peas (mangetout),
cut into thin strips
185 g/6 oz Camembert cheese, sliced
185 g/6 oz raspberries
60 g/2 oz raw almonds, roasted

MUSTARD MARINADE
1 tablespoon grated fresh ginger
1 tablespoon wholegrain mustard
1 clove garlic, crushed
$^1/_4$ cup/60 mL/2 fl oz plum sauce
1 tablespoon raspberry or
white wine vinegar
1 tablespoon vegetable oil

ORANGE DRESSING
$^1/_4$ cup/60 mL/2 fl oz orange juice
2 tablespoons vegetable oil
1 tablespoon raspberry vinegar
1 tablespoon Dijon mustard

Mizuna lettuce has a long
thin jagged leaf and makes
a pretty base for this salad.
If it is unavailable any soft
leaf lettuce of your choice
is a suitable alternative.

1   To make marinade, place ginger, mustard, garlic, plum sauce, vinegar and oil in a shallow glass or ceramic dish and mix to combine. Add duck and onions, turn to coat, cover and marinate in the refrigerator for 4 hours.

2   Preheat barbecue to a medium heat. Drain duck and onions well and reserve marinade. Place duck and onions on lightly oiled barbecue plate (griddle) and cook, basting frequently with reserved marinade and turning occasionally, for 10 minutes or until duck is tender. Set aside to cool slightly, then cut duck into thin slices.

3   Line a serving platter with lettuce and snow peas (mangetout), top with duck, onions, Camembert cheese, raspberries and almonds and toss gently to combine.

4   To make dressing, place orange juice, oil, vinegar and mustard in a bowl and whisk to combine. Drizzle dressing over salad and serve immediately.

Serves 6

Plum Duck Salad

Chicken Pesto Burgers

CHICKEN PESTO BURGERS

4 rolls, slit and toasted
125 g/4 oz rocket or watercress
1 tomato, sliced

CHICKEN PESTO PATTIES
$^1/_2$ bunch fresh basil
2 tablespoons pine nuts
1 tablespoon grated Parmesan cheese
1 clove garlic, crushed
2 tablespoons olive oil
500 g/1 lb chicken mince
1 cup/60 g/2 oz breadcrumbs, made
from stale bread
1 red pepper, roasted and diced
1 onion, diced
1 egg white
freshly ground black pepper

1   Preheat barbecue to a medium heat.
To make patties, place basil leaves, pine
nuts, Parmesan cheese, garlic and oil in
a food processor or blender and process
until smooth. Transfer mixture to a
bowl, add chicken, breadcrumbs, red
pepper, onion, egg white and black
pepper to taste and mix well to
combine.

2   Shape chicken mixture into four
patties. Place patties on lightly oiled
barbecue plate (griddle) and cook for
3 minutes each side or until cooked.

3   To serve, top bottom half of each
roll with rocket or watercress, then
with a pattie, tomato slices and top half
of roll. Serve immediately.

Serves 4

Peppers are easy to roast
on the barbecue, remove
seeds cut into quarters and
place skin side down on a
preheated hot barbecue.
Cook until skins are charred
and blistered, then place in
a plastic food bag or paper
bag and set aside until cool
enough to handle. Remove
skin and use as desired.

BUFFALO CHILLI CHICKEN

1 kg/2 lb chicken pieces, skinned
3 spring onions, chopped
2 cloves garlic, crushed
1 cup/250 mL/8 fl oz tomato sauce
$^1/_4$ cup/60 mL/2 fl oz beer
1 tablespoon cider vinegar
1 tablespoon honey
1 tablespoon Tabasco sauce or
according to taste

The cooking times for the chicken will vary according to the size of the pieces. If you have a variety of sizes, place the larger, longer cooking pieces such as drumsticks and thighs on the barbecue first and cook for 5 minutes, before adding the smaller quicker cooking pieces such as wings and breasts.

1   Score larger pieces of chicken at 2 cm/$^3/_4$ in intervals and set aside.

2   Place spring onions, garlic, tomato sauce, beer, vinegar, honey and Tabasco sauce in a shallow glass or ceramic dish and mix to combine. Add chicken, toss to coat, cover and marinate in the refrigerator for 3-4 hours.

3   Preheat barbecue to a medium heat. Drain chicken and reserve marinade. Place chicken on lightly oiled barbecue grill and cook, basting frequently with reserved marinade and turning several times, for 10-15 minutes or until chicken is tender and cooked through.

Serves 4

CHILLI LIME LEGS

$^1/_4$ cup/60 mL/2 fl oz lime juice
$^1/_4$ cup/60 mL/2 fl oz buttermilk
2 tablespoons sweet chilli sauce
2 tablespoons reduced-salt soy sauce
12 chicken drumsticks, skinned

Buttermilk, which has a similar nutritional value to skim milk, is mildly acidic with a creamy taste and a thick consistency. A mixture of 2 tablespoons low-fat natural yogurt and 1 tablespoon reduced-fat milk can be used instead.

1   Place lime juice, buttermilk, chilli sauce and soy sauce in a shallow glass or ceramic dish and mix to combine. Score each drumstick in several places, add to lime juice mixture, turn to coat, cover and marinate in the refrigerator for 3 hours.

2   Preheat barbecue to a medium heat. Drain chicken well and reserve marinade. Place chicken on lightly oiled barbecue grill and cook, basting frequently with reserved marinade and turning occasionally, for 25 minutes or until chicken is cooked.

Serves 6

Chilli Lime Legs, Buffalo Chilli Chicken

MAKE MINE MEAT

Red meat is one of the most popular barbecue foods. Here you will find new ways to make the most of your favourite cuts. Why not try Cajun Spiced Steaks or Californian Pork Kebabs at your next barbecue?

LAMB WITH HONEYED ONIONS

12 lamb cutlets, trimmed of excess fat

YOGURT MARINADE
1 tablespoon chopped fresh mint
1 clove garlic, crushed
1 cup/200 g/6^1/$_2$ oz low-fat
natural yogurt
2 tablespoons wholegrain mustard
1 tablespoon prepared mint sauce

HONEYED ONIONS
2 tablespoons olive oil
2 red onions, sliced
1 tablespoon honey
2 tablespoons red wine vinegar

1   To make marinade, place mint,
garlic, yogurt, mustard and mint sauce
in a shallow glass or ceramic dish and
mix to combine. Add lamb, turn to
coat, cover and marinate in the
refrigerator for 3 hours.

2   Preheat barbecue to a medium heat.
For Honeyed Onions, heat oil on
barbecue plate (griddle), add onions
and cook, stirring constantly, for
10 minutes. Add honey and vinegar
and cook, stirring, for 5 minutes longer
or until onions are very soft and golden.

3   Drain lamb, place on lightly oiled
barbecue and cook for 2-3 minutes
each side or until cooked to your
liking. Serve with onions.

Serves 6

Before lighting a gas
barbecue check that all
the gas fittings and hose
connections are tight and
fitting correctly.

STEAKS WITH BLUE BUTTER

1 tablespoon freshly ground
black pepper
2 tablespoons olive oil
6 fillet steaks, trimmed of excess fat

BLUE BUTTER
125 g/4 oz butter, softened
60 g/2 oz blue cheese
1 tablespoon chopped fresh parsley
1 teaspoon paprika

1   To make Blue Butter, place butter,
blue cheese, parsley and paprika in a
bowl and beat to combine. Place butter
on a piece of plastic food wrap and roll
into a log shape. Refrigerate for 1 hour
or until firm.

2   Preheat barbecue to a high heat.

3   Place black pepper and oil in a bowl
and mix to combine. Brush steaks
lightly with oil mixture. Place steaks on
lightly oiled barbecue grill and cook for
3-5 minutes each side or until steaks
are cooked to your liking.

4   Cut butter into 2 cm/^{3}/4 in thick
slices and top each steak with
1 or 2 slices. Serve immediately.

Serves 6

Any leftover Blue Butter can
be stored in the freezer to
use at a later date. It is also
delicious served with grilled
lamb chops or cutlets and
grilled vegetables such as
eggplant (aubergine), red
and green peppers and
zucchini (courgettes).

THAI LAMB AND NOODLE SALAD

1 stalk fresh lemon grass, chopped or
$^1/_2$ teaspoon dried lemon grass, soaked
in hot water until soft
2 cloves garlic, crushed
$^1/_4$ cup/60 mL/2 fl oz lime juice
2 tablespoons vegetable oil
2 tablespoons sweet chilli sauce
1 tablespoon fish sauce
750 g/1$^1/_2$ lb lamb fillets, trimmed of
excess fat and sinew

RICE NOODLE SALAD
155 g/5 oz rice noodles
6 spring onions, chopped
1 red pepper, chopped
60 g/2 oz bean sprouts
3 tablespoons fresh coriander leaves

LIME AND CHILLI DRESSING
$^1/_4$ cup/60 mL/2 fl oz lime juice
1 tablespoon fish sauce
1 tablespoon honey
pinch chilli powder or
according to taste

1 Combine lemon grass, garlic, lime juice, oil, chilli sauce and fish sauce in a glass or ceramic dish and mix to combine. Add lamb, turn to coat, cover and marinate in the refrigerator for 3 hours.

2 Preheat barbecue to a medium heat. To make salad, prepare noodles according to packet directions. Drain and place in a bowl. Add spring onions, red pepper, bean sprouts and coriander and toss to combine. Set aside.

3 To make dressing, place lime juice, fish sauce, honey and chilli powder in a screwtop jar and shake well to combine. Set aside.

4 Drain lamb and cook on lightly oiled barbecue, turning several times, for 5-10 minutes or until cooked to your liking. Slice lamb diagonally into 2 cm/$^3/_4$ in thick slices.

5 To serve, place salad on a large serving platter, arrange lamb attractively on top and drizzle with dressing. Serve immediately.

Serves 6

Rice noodles, also called rice vermicelli or rice sticks, vary in size from a narrow vermicelli style to a ribbon noodle about 5 mm/$^1/_4$ in wide. Made from rice flour, the noodles should be soaked before using; the narrow noodles require about 10 minutes soaking, while the wider ones will need about 30 minutes.

Steaks with Blue Butter

BEEF AND BACON BURGERS

750 g/1¹/₂ lb lean beef mince
3 spring onions, chopped
2 tablespoons snipped fresh chives
1 egg, lightly beaten
2 tablespoons tomato sauce
1 tablespoon Worcestershire sauce
1 tablespoon chilli sauce
125 g/4 oz grated mozzarella cheese
6 rashers bacon, rind removed

1 Preheat barbecue to a medium heat. Place beef, spring onions, chives, egg, tomato sauce, Worcestershire sauce and chilli sauce in a bowl and mix to combine. Shape mixture into twelve patties. Top six patties with mozzarella cheese, then with remaining patties and pinch edges together to seal. Wrap a piece of bacon around each pattie and secure with a wooden toothpick or cocktail stick. Place on a plate and refrigerate for 2 hours or until patties are firm.

2 Place patties in a lightly oiled hinged wire barbecue frame and cook on barbecue grill for 10-15 minutes or until patties are cooked to your liking and cheese melts.

A hinged wire frame is a useful barbecue accessory. It is ideal for cooking fragile and delicate foods such as fish – whole, fillets and cutlets – and burgers which can fall apart when turning.

Serves 6

Plate Villeroy & Boch

ORIENTAL PORK RIBS

Left: Beef and Bacon Burgers
Above: Oriental Pork Ribs

1.5 kg/3 lb pork spareribs
2 cloves garlic, crushed
1 tablespoon finely grated fresh ginger
1 tablespoon chopped fresh coriander
1 teaspoon five spice powder
$^1/_4$ cup/60 mL/2 fl oz soy sauce
2 tablespoons sweet chilli sauce
2 tablespoons hoisin sauce
1 tablespoon tomato sauce
1 tablespoon sherry
1 teaspoon rice vinegar

1 Place ribs on a wire rack set in a baking dish and bake for $1^1/_2$ hours. Set aside to cool slightly.

2 Preheat barbecue to a medium heat. Place garlic, ginger, coriander, five spice powder, soy sauce, chilli sauce, hoisin sauce, tomato sauce, sherry and vinegar in a bowl and mix to combine. Add ribs and toss to coat.

3 Drain ribs and reserve liquid. Place ribs on lightly oiled barbecue plate (griddle) and cook, turning and basting frequently with reserved liquid, for 10 minutes or until ribs are tender.

Serves 6

Oven temperature
180°C, 350°F, Gas 4

Five spice powder is a pungent, fragrant, spicy and slightly sweet powder which is a mixture of star anise, fennel, Szechuan peppercorns, cloves and cinnamon. It adds a delicate anise flavour to foods.

41

HERBED AND SPICED PORK LOIN

Oven temperature
190°C, 375°F, Gas 5

This recipe can be cooked
in a covered barbecue,
in which case it is not
necessary to precook the
pork in the oven. If cooking
in a covered barbecue
preheat the barbecue to a
medium heat and cook for
2-2¹/₂ hours. When scoring
the rind take care not to
cut through into the flesh.

2 kg/4 lb boneless pork loin, rolled
and rind scored at 2 cm/³/4 in intervals

HERB AND SPICE MARINADE
1 onion, chopped
2 tablespoons crushed pink
peppercorns
2 tablespoons crushed green
peppercorns
2 tablespoons ground coriander
1 tablespoon freshly ground
black pepper
1 tablespoon ground cumin
1 teaspoon garam masala
1 teaspoon ground mixed spice
1 teaspoon turmeric
1 teaspoon paprika
1 teaspoon sea salt
2 tablespoons peanut oil
2 tablespoons sesame oil
1 tablespoon white vinegar

1   To make marinade, place onion,
pink peppercorns, green peppercorns,
coriander, black pepper, cumin, garam
masala, mixed spice, turmeric, paprika,
salt, peanut oil, sesame oil and vinegar
into a food processor or blender and
process to make a paste.

2   Rub marinade over pork, place in a
glass or ceramic dish, cover and
marinate in the refrigerator overnight.

3   Place pork on a wire rack set in a
baking dish and bake for 1 hour.
Preheat barbecue to a medium heat.
Transfer pork to lightly oiled barbecue
grill and cook, turning frequently, for
1¹/₂ hours or until pork is tender and
cooked through. Stand for 10 minutes
before carving and serving.

Serves 8

CALIFORNIAN PORK KEBABS

500 g/1 lb pork fillets, cut
into 2 cm/³/4 in cubes
1 small pineapple, cut into
2 cm/³/4 in cubes

PINEAPPLE MARINADE
1 onion, chopped
3 cloves garlic, chopped
2 dried red chillies
2 tablespoons chopped fresh thyme
2 tablespoons chopped fresh oregano
2 teaspoons ground cumin
2 teaspoons freshly ground
black pepper
¹/3 cup/90 mL/3 fl oz lemon juice
¹/3 cup/90 mL/3 fl oz pineapple juice
2 tablespoons olive oil

As most marinades contain
an acid ingredient, such as
lemon juice, vinegar, soy
sauce or wine, marinating is
best done in a glass,
ceramic, stainless steel or
enamel dish. Deep-sided
disposable aluminium
dishes are also good for
marinating.

1   To make marinade, place onion,
garlic, chillies, thyme, oregano, cumin,
black pepper, lemon juice, pineapple
juice and oil into a food processor or
blender and process until smooth.

2   Place pork in a glass or ceramic
bowl, pour over marinade and toss to
combine. Cover and marinate at room
temperature for 2 hours or in the
refrigerator overnight.

3   Preheat barbecue to a medium heat.
Drain pork well. Thread pork and
pineapple, alternately, onto lightly
oiled skewers. Place skewers on lightly
oiled barbecue grill and cook, turning
several times, for 5-8 minutes or until
pork is tender and cooked through.

Serves 6

Bow/s Accoutrement

Above: Korean Bulgogi
Right: Barbecued Lamb Pitta Breads

KOREAN BULGOGI

4 cloves garlic, crushed
2 teaspoons finely grated fresh ginger
$^1/_4$ cup/60 mL/2 fl oz soy sauce
3 tablespoons honey
1 tablespoon sweet chilli sauce
750 g/1$^1/_2$ lb rump steak, trimmed of visible fat and thinly sliced
2 tablespoons vegetable oil
2 onions, sliced
125 g/4 oz bean sprouts
2 tablespoons sesame seeds

1   Place garlic, ginger, soy sauce, honey and chilli sauce in a bowl and mix to combine. Add beef, toss to coat, cover and marinate in the refrigerator for 4 hours.

2   Preheat barbecue to a high heat. Heat 1 tablespoon oil on barbecue plate (griddle), add beef and stir-fry for 1-2 minutes or until beef just changes colour. Push beef to side of barbecue to keep warm.

3   Heat remaining oil on barbecue plate (griddle), add onions and bean sprouts and stir-fry for 4-5 minutes or until onions are golden. Add beef to onion mixture and stir-fry for 1-2 minutes longer. Sprinkle with sesame seeds and serve immediately.

Serve with steamed white or brown rice and a tossed green salad.

Serves 6

44

BARBECUED LAMB PITTA BREADS

1 tablespoon finely grated lemon rind
1 teaspoon ground cumin
1 tablespoon olive oil
750 g/1^{1}/$_{2}$ lb lamb fillets
6 pitta bread rounds
6 tablespoons ready-made hummus
1 bunch curly endive
250 g/8 oz ready-made tabbouleh

Serves 6

1   Combine lemon rind, cumin and oil. Rub surface of lamb with oil mixture, place in a shallow glass or ceramic dish and marinate at room temperature for 30 minutes.

2   Preheat barbecue to a medium heat. Place lamb on lightly oiled barbecue grill and cook for 3-5 minutes each side or until lamb is tender and cooked to your liking. Stand for 2 minutes before slicing.

3   Warm pitta breads on barbecue for 1-2 minutes each side. Split each pitta bread to make a pocket, then spread with hummus and fill with endive, tabbouleh and sliced lamb.

Tabbouleh is a parsley and burghul (cracked wheat) salad and is available from some delicatessens and larger supermarkets.

FRUITY BARBECUED LAMB

Oven temperature
180°C, 350°F, Gas 4

Use fresh young garlic for this recipe, its flavour is milder than more mature garlic and when cooked develops a delicious nutty taste. Lamb chops are also delicious cooked in this way, however no precooking is required and the cooking time on the barbecue will only be 3-5 minutes each side.

4 lamb shanks (knuckles)
2 tablespoons mango chutney
2 cloves garlic, crushed
1 tablespoon finely grated fresh ginger
$^1/_4$ cup/60 mL/2 fl oz apple juice
$^1/_4$ cup/60 ml/2 fl oz white wine
2 tablespoons olive oil
4 bulbs young garlic, cut in half horizontally

1 Score the thickest part of each lamb shank (knuckle) to allow for even cooking.

2 Place chutney, crushed garlic, ginger, apple juice, wine and oil in a shallow ovenproof glass, ceramic or enamel dish and mix to combine. Add lamb, turn to coat, cover and marinate in the refrigerator for 2 hours. Remove lamb from refrigerator and bake in oven for 1 hour.

3 Preheat barbecue to a medium heat. Remove lamb from baking dish and place on lightly oiled barbecue, add garlic bulbs and cook, turning occasionally, for 30 minutes or until lamb and garlic are tender.

Serves 4

ROSEMARY AND THYME CHOPS

12 lamb neck chops, trimmed of excess fat

FRESH HERB MARINADE
2 tablespoons chopped fresh rosemary
2 tablespoons chopped fresh thyme
2 cloves garlic, crushed
$^1/_4$ cup/60 mL/2 fl oz olive oil
$^1/_4$ cup/60 mL/2 fl oz balsamic or red wine vinegar
2 tablespoons lime juice

1 To make marinade, place rosemary, thyme, garlic, oil, vinegar and lime juice in a shallow glass or ceramic dish and mix to combine. Add lamb, turn to coat, cover and marinate at room temperature for 1 hour.

2 Preheat barbecue to a high heat. Drain lamb, place on lightly oiled barbecue and cook for 3-5 minutes each side or until chops are cooked to your liking.

Serves 6

Long-handled tongs are a must for turning food without burning your hands.

Fruity Barbecued Lamb, Rosemary and Thyme Chops

CAJUN SPICED STEAKS

When testing to see if a steak is cooked to your liking, press it with a pair of blunt tongs. Do not cut the meat, as this causes the juices to escape. Rare steaks will feel springy, medium steaks slightly springy and well-done steaks will feel firm. As a guide a 2.5 cm/1 in thick steak cooked to rare takes about 3 minutes each side, a medium steak 4 minutes and a well-done steak 5 minutes.

4 sirloin or fillet steaks, trimmed of excess fat

CAJUN SPICE MIXTURE
1 tablespoon sweet paprika
1 teaspoon crushed black peppercorns
1 teaspoon ground thyme
1 teaspoon ground oregano
$^1/_4$ teaspoon chilli powder

PINEAPPLE CHILLI SALSA
$^1/_2$ pineapple, peeled and chopped
2 spring onions, chopped
1 tablespoon chopped fresh coriander
1 fresh red chilli, chopped
1 tablespoon brown sugar
1 tablespoon white vinegar

1 Preheat barbecue to a high heat. To make salsa, place pineapple, spring onions, coriander, chilli, sugar and vinegar in a bowl and toss to combine. Set aside.

2 To make spice mixture, combine paprika, black peppercorns, thyme, oregano and chilli powder. Rub spice mixture over steaks. Place steaks on lightly oiled barbecue and cook for 3-5 minutes each side or until cooked to your liking. Serve with salsa.

Serves 4

Plate Villeroy & Boch

PORK SKEWERS WITH SALSA

Left: Cajun Spiced Steaks
Above: Pork Skewers with Salsa

500 g/1 lb lean pork mince
1 cup/60 g/2 oz breadcrumbs, made
from stale bread
1 onion, chopped
2 cloves garlic, crushed
1 tablespoon chopped oregano
1 teaspoon ground cumin
$^1/_2$ teaspoon chilli powder
1 egg, lightly beaten

ARTICHOKE SALSA
1 tablespoon olive oil
1 onion, chopped
185 g/6 oz marinated artichoke
hearts, chopped
4 tomatoes, seeded and chopped
2 tablespoons tomato paste (purée)
1 tablespoon chopped fresh oregano

1 Place pork, breadcrumbs, onion,
garlic, oregano, cumin, chilli powder
and egg in a bowl and mix to combine.

2 Shape tablespoons of pork mixture
into balls, place on a plate lined with
plastic food wrap, cover and refrigerate
for 30 minutes.

3 Preheat barbecue to a medium heat.
Thread four balls onto a lightly oiled
skewer. Repeat with remaining balls.
Place skewers on lightly oiled barbecue
grill and cook, turning frequently, for
8 minutes or until cooked through.

4 To make salsa, heat oil in a frying
pan over a medium heat, add onion and
cook, stirring, for 3 minutes or until
onion is golden. Add artichokes,
tomatoes, tomato paste (purée) and
oregano and cook, stirring, for
3-4 minutes longer or until heated
through. Serve with skewers.

Serves 4

These skewers can also be
made using a combination
of pork and veal mince.

49

MEATLESS MAIN EVENTS

Given the number of people who now choose to be vegetarians or semi-vegetarians it is a good idea to serve a vegetarian alternative – these recipes fit the bill and are sure to be popular with everyone.

GRILLED PEPPER AND PESTO PIZZA

1 quantity Basic Pizza Dough
(page 54)

PEPPER AND PESTO TOPPING
2 red peppers, seeded and cut
into quarters
2 green peppers, seeded and cut
into quarters
2 yellow peppers, seeded and cut
into quarters
4 baby eggplant (aubergines), halved
lengthwise
2 tablespoons olive oil
3/4 cup/185 g/6 oz ready-made pesto
90 g/3 oz grated Parmesan cheese

Pizzas are always popular and nothing could be more delicious than these barbecued pizzas. Once you have mastered the pizzas in this chapter try some of your own ideas using your favourite ingredients for topping.

1 Preheat barbecue to a high heat. To make topping, brush red peppers, green peppers, yellow peppers and eggplant (aubergines) with oil and cook on barbecue grill for 3-4 minutes each side or until vegetables are soft and golden. Set aside.

2 Divide dough into four portions and roll into rounds 3 mm/^{1}/8 in thick. Place dough rounds on lightly oiled barbecue and cook for 3-5 minutes or until brown and crisp. Turn over, spread with pesto, top with roasted peppers and eggplant (aubergine) and sprinkle with Parmesan cheese. Cook for 4-6 minutes longer or until pizza crust is crisp, golden and cooked through. Serve immediately.

Serves 4

BARBECUED TOFU BRUSCHETTA

500 g/1 lb firm tofu
3 tablespoons olive oil
2 cloves garlic, crushed
1 small French bread stick, cut
into 12 slices
3 tablespoons chopped fresh coriander

CHILLI MARINADE
^{1}/3 cup/90 mL/3 fl oz vegetable stock
3 tablespoons Japanese soy sauce
2 teaspoons sesame oil
2 teaspoons chilli sauce

Do not barbecue in enclosed areas. If wet weather has forced you to move your barbecue undercover, ensure there is plenty of ventilation. For more information about Japanese soy sauce see hint on page 14.

1 To make marinade place stock, soy sauce, sesame oil and chilli sauce in a shallow glass or ceramic dish and mix to combine. Cut tofu into 12 pieces, add to marinade, toss to coat, cover and marinate at room temperature for 1 hour.

2 Preheat barbecue to a medium heat. Combine olive oil and garlic, brush over bread slices, place on lightly oiled barbecue grill and cook for 2-3 minutes each side or until golden.

3 Drain tofu and cook on barbecue for 2-3 minutes each side or until golden. Place a piece of tofu on each bruschetta, sprinkle with coriander and serve immediately.

Makes 12

Wild Rice and Bean Patties

WILD RICE AND BEAN PATTIES

440 g/14 oz canned soya beans,
drained and rinsed
6 tablespoons chopped fresh coriander
3 spring onions, chopped
1 tablespoon finely grated fresh ginger
1 tablespoon ground cumin
1 tablespoon ground coriander
$^1/_2$ teaspoon ground turmeric
$^1/_2$ cup/100 g/3$^1/_2$ oz wild rice blend,
cooked
$^1/_2$ cup/75 g/2$^1/_2$ oz wholemeal flour
1 egg, lightly beaten
2 tablespoons vegetable oil

SWEET CHILLI YOGURT
1 cup/200 g/6$^1/_2$ oz low-fat
natural yogurt
2 tablespoons sweet chilli sauce
1 tablespoon lime juice

1 Preheat barbecue to a medium heat. Place soya beans, fresh coriander, spring onions, ginger, cumin, ground coriander and turmeric into a food processor and process for 30 seconds or until mixture resembles coarse breadcrumbs. Transfer mixture to a bowl, add rice, flour and egg and mix to combine. Shape mixture into patties.

2 Heat oil on barbecue plate (griddle) for 2-3 minutes or until hot, add patties and cook for 5 minutes each side or until golden and heated through.

3 To make chilli yogurt, place yogurt, chilli sauce and lime juice in a bowl and mix to combine. Serve with patties.

Serves 6

For more information on wild rice blend see hint on page 18.

Plate Villeroy & Boch

BASIC PIZZA DOUGH

1 teaspoon active dry yeast
pinch sugar
$^2/_3$ cup/170 mL/5$^1/_2$ fl oz warm water
2 cups/250 g/8 oz flour
$^1/_2$ teaspoon salt
$^1/_4$ cup/60 mL/2 fl oz olive oil

There are two types of yeast commonly used in bread-making – fresh and dry. Dry yeast is twice as concentrated as fresh yeast. You will find that 15 g/$^1/_2$ oz dry yeast has the same raising power as 30 g/1 oz fresh yeast.

1   Place yeast, sugar and water in a bowl and mix to dissolve. Set aside in a warm, draught-free place for 5 minutes or until mixture is foamy.

2   Place flour and salt in a food processor and pulse once or twice to sift. With machine running, slowly pour in yeast mixture and oil and process to form a rough dough. Turn dough onto a lightly floured surface and knead for 5 minutes or until soft and shiny. Add more flour if necessary.

3   Place dough in a lightly oiled large bowl, roll dough around bowl to cover surface with oil. Cover bowl with plastic food wrap and place in a warm draught-free place for 1-1$^1/_2$ hours or until doubled in size. Knock down, knead lightly and use as desired.

Makes enough dough for 4 individual pizzas or 1 large pizza

NUTTY-CRUSTED RICOTTA SALAD

315 g/10 oz ricotta cheese in one piece
90 g/3 oz grated Parmesan cheese
60 g/2 oz pine nuts, toasted and finely chopped
1 tablespoon sweet paprika
1 tablespoon dried oregano
4 tablespoons olive oil
315 g/10 oz assorted salad leaves
90 g/3 oz snow pea (mangetout) sprouts or watercress
185 g/6 oz yellow teardrop or cherry tomatoes
1 avocado, stoned, peeled and chopped
30 g/1 oz sun-dried tomatoes, sliced

SPICED HONEY DRESSING
2 cloves garlic, crushed
1 teaspoon ground cumin
1 teaspoon ground coriander
pinch red chilli flakes
$^1/_4$ cup/60 mL/2 fl oz olive oil
1 tablespoon cider vinegar
1 teaspoon honey

If a gas barbecue does not light first time, turn if off, wait 20 seconds and try again. This will ensure that there is no gas build-up.

1   Place ricotta cheese in a colander lined with muslin and drain for 1 hour.

2   Preheat barbecue to a medium heat. Place Parmesan cheese, pine nuts, paprika, oregano and 2 tablespoons oil in a bowl and mix to combine. Press nut mixture over surface of ricotta cheese to coat.

3   Heat remaining oil on barbecue plate (griddle) until hot, then cook ricotta cheese, turning occasionally, for 10 minutes or until golden. Stand for 10 minutes, then cut into slices.

4   Line a large serving platter with salad leaves, then arrange snow pea (mangetout) sprouts or watercress, teardrop or cherry tomatoes, avocado, sun-dried tomatoes and ricotta cheese slices attractively on top.

5   To make dressing, place garlic, cumin, coriander, chilli flakes, oil, vinegar and honey in a bowl and whisk to combine. Drizzle over salad and serve.

Serves 4

Nutty-crusted Ricotta Salad

BARBECUED PUMPKIN PIZZA

**1 quantity Basic Pizza Dough
(page 54)**

PUMPKIN AND FETA TOPPING
**1 tablespoon olive oil
8 large slices pumpkin, peeled and
seeds removed
1 onion, sliced
315 g/10 oz feta cheese, crumbled
1 tablespoon chopped fresh thyme
freshly ground black pepper**

Orange sweet potatoes
make a delicious alternative
to the pumpkin in this recipe.

1 Preheat barbecue to a high heat.
To make topping, heat oil on barbecue
plate (griddle) for 2-3 minutes or until
hot, add pumpkin and onion and cook
for 5 minutes each side or until soft and
golden. Set aside.

2 Divide dough into four portions and
roll into rounds 3 mm/^{1}/8 in thick.
Place dough rounds on lightly oiled
barbecue and cook for 3-5 minutes or
until brown and crisp. Turn over, top
with pumpkin, onion, feta cheese,
thyme and black pepper to taste and
cook for 4-6 minutes longer or until
pizza crust is crisp, golden and cooked
through. Serve immediately.

Serves 4

Couscous-filled Mushrooms

Left: Barbecued Pumpkin Pizza
Above: Couscous-filled Mushrooms

²/₃ cup/125 g/4 oz couscous
²/₃ cup/170 mL/5¹/₂ fl oz boiling water
15 g/¹/₂ oz butter
2 teaspoons olive oil
1 onion, chopped
2 cloves garlic, crushed
1 teaspoon garam masala
pinch cayenne pepper
12 large mushrooms, stalks removed
200 g/6¹/₂ oz feta cheese, crumbled

Serves 4

1   Preheat barbecue to a high heat. Place couscous in a bowl, pour over boiling water, cover and set aside to stand for 5 minutes or until water is absorbed. Add butter and toss gently with a fork.

2   Heat oil in a frying pan over a medium heat, add onion and garlic and cook, stirring, for 3 minutes or until onion is soft. Add garam masala and cayenne pepper and cook for 1 minute longer. Add onion mixture to couscous and toss to combine.

3   Fill mushrooms with couscous mixture, top with feta cheese and cook on lightly oiled barbecue grill for 5 minutes or until mushrooms are tender and cheese melts.

If your barbecue only has a grill, use a large long-handled frying pan when a recipe calls for food to be cooked on the barbecue plate (griddle).

WARM VEGETABLE SALAD

6 zucchini (courgettes), cut
lengthwise into quarters
2 red onions, sliced
155 g/5 oz snow pea (mangetout)
sprouts or watercress
1 yellow or red pepper, chopped
1 avocado, stoned, peeled and chopped

ORANGE DRESSING
2 tablespoons snipped fresh chives
$1/4$ cup/60 mL/2 fl oz orange juice
1 tablespoon white wine vinegar
2 teaspoons French mustard

1   Preheat barbecue to a medium heat.
Place zucchini (courgettes) and onions
on lightly oiled barbecue and cook for
2-3 minutes each side or until golden
and tender.

2   Arrange snow pea (mangetout)
sprouts or watercress, yellow or red
pepper and avocado attractively on a
serving platter. Top with zucchini
(courgettes) and onions.

3   To make dressing, place chives,
orange juice, vinegar and mustard in a
screwtop jar and shake well to combine.
Drizzle over salad and serve immediately.

Serves 4

This salad is delicious served
with toasted olive bread.

KEBABS WITH HERB SAUCE

1 green pepper, seeded and cut into
2 cm/^{3}/4 in squares
2 zucchini (courgettes), cut into
2 cm/^{3}/4 in pieces
1 red onion, cut into 2 cm/^{3}/4 in cubes
1 eggplant (aubergine), cut into
2 cm/^{3}/4 in cubes
16 cherry tomatoes
2 tablespoons olive oil
2 tablespoons lemon juice
1 tablespoon chopped fresh oregano or
1 teaspoon dried oregano

HERB SAUCE
1 tablespoon chopped fresh dill
2 tablespoons snipped fresh chives
1 cup/250 g/8 oz sour cream
2 tablespoons lemon juice

1   Preheat barbecue to a medium heat.
Thread a piece of green pepper,
zucchini (courgette), onion, eggplant
(aubergine) and a tomato onto a lightly
oiled skewer. Repeat with remaining
vegetables to use all ingredients.

2   Combine oil, lemon juice and
oregano and brush over kebabs. Place
kebabs on lightly oiled barbecue grill
and cook, turning several times, for
5-10 minutes or until vegetables are
tender.

3   To make sauce, place dill, chives,
sour cream and lemon juice in a bowl
and mix to combine. Serve with
kebabs.

Serves 4

Always keep water close
at hand when barbecuing.
If a hose or tap is not close
by, then have a bucket of
water next to the barbecue.
A fire extinguisher or fire
blanket is also a sensible
safety precaution.

Warm Vegetable Salad, Kebabs with Herb Sauce

UNDERCOVER COOKING

When used uncovered the kettle or covered barbecue is just like any other barbecue, however add the cover or lid and you have a piece of equipment that roasts and smokes food to perfection.

Previous pages: Slow-roasted Leg of Lamb, Barbecued Vegetables

SLOW-ROASTED LEG OF LAMB

1.5 kg/3 lb leg of lamb
3 cloves garlic, thinly sliced

FRESH HERB MARINADE
4 tablespoons chopped fresh rosemary
4 tablespoons chopped fresh mint
1/2 cup/125 mL/4 fl oz white
wine vinegar
1/4 cup/60 mL/2 fl oz olive oil
freshly ground black pepper

1 To make marinade, place rosemary, mint, vinegar, oil and black pepper to taste in a bowl and mix to combine.

2 Cut several deep slits in the surface of the lamb. Fill each slit with a slice of garlic. Place lamb in a glass or ceramic dish, pour over marinade, turn to coat, cover and marinate in the refrigerator for 4 hours.

3 Preheat covered barbecue to a medium heat. Place lamb on a wire rack set in a roasting tin and pour over marinade. Place roasting tin on rack in barbecue, cover barbecue with lid and cook, basting occasionally, for 1 1/2-2 hours or until lamb is tender. Cover and stand for 15 minutes before carving.

Serves 6

Disposable aluminium foil dishes sold in supermarkets as turkey roasting dishes are ideal for cooking larger pieces of meat in the kettle or covered barbecue. They save on clean-up and your good roasting tin is preserved.

BARBECUED VEGETABLES

315 g/10 oz sweet potato, peeled and
cut into 3 cm/1 1/4 in thick slices
315 g/10 oz pumpkin, peeled and
cut into wedges
6 medium potatoes, halved
12 baby onions
6 carrots, peeled
6 parsnips, peeled
6 baby beetroot, peeled
1/4 cup/60 mL/2 fl oz olive oil
4 sprigs fresh lemon thyme or thyme
4 sprigs fresh rosemary

1 Preheat covered barbecue to a medium heat. Bring a saucepan of water to the boil, add sweet potato, pumpkin and potatoes and cook for 10 minutes, drain well.

2 Place sweet potato, pumpkin, potatoes, onions, carrots, parsnips and beetroot on a lightly oiled baking tray. Brush vegetables lightly with oil and scatter with sprigs of thyme and rosemary.

3 Place baking tray on rack in barbecue, cover barbecue with lid and cook for 40 minutes or until vegetables are tender.

Serves 6

For a special family celebration Slow-roasted Leg of Lamb, Barbecued Vegetables and Mixed Leaf Salad (page 80) makes a meal that is sure to be remembered long after the event. For dessert Summer Berry Jelly (page 78) served with cream or ice cream is the perfect way to end the meal.

Home-smoked Trout

HOME-SMOKED TROUT

1 cup/125 g/4 oz smoking chips
$^1/_2$ cup/125 mL/4 fl oz white wine
4 small rainbow trout, cleaned, with
head and tail intact
1 tablespoon vegetable oil
3 red onions, thinly sliced
1 lemon, thinly sliced
8 sprigs dill

1   Place smoking chips and wine in a
non-reactive metal dish and stand for
1 hour.

2   Preheat covered barbecue to a low
heat. Place dish, with smoking chips in,
in barbecue over hot coals, cover
barbecue with lid and heat for
5-10 minutes or until liquid is hot.

3   Place trout on a wire rack set in a
roasting tin. Brush trout lightly with
oil, then top with onions, lemon and
dill. Position roasting tin containing
trout on rack in barbecue, cover
barbecue with lid and smoke for
15-20 minutes or until trout flakes
when tested with fork.

Serves 4

This recipe is also suitable
for a smoke box.

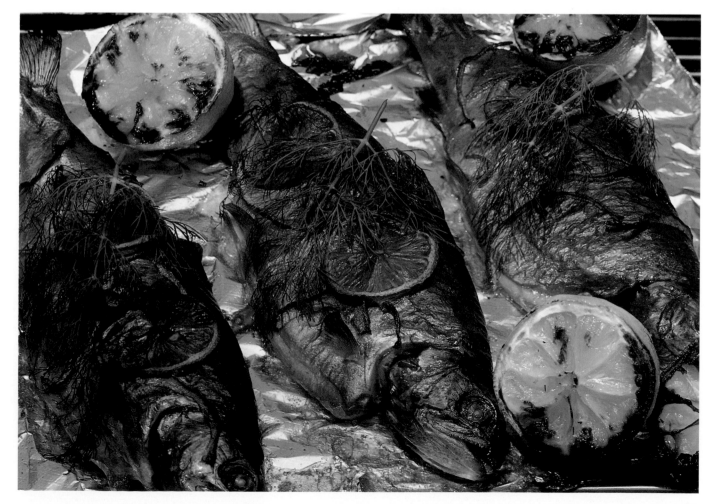

GATHER ROUND DAMPER

2 cups/250 g/8 oz self-raising flour
1 cup/155 g/5 oz wholemeal
self-raising flour
60 g/2 oz butter, chopped
1 egg, lightly beaten
1 cup/250 mL/8 fl oz milk

Opposite: Festive Smoked Turkey

Serve damper as a savoury bread accompanied by chutneys and relishes with the main meal or as a sweet finish with butter and golden syrup.

1   Preheat covered barbecue to a medium heat. Sift together flour and wholemeal flour into a bowl, return husks to bowl. Rub in butter, using fingertips until mixture resembles fine breadcrumbs. Make a well in the centre of the mixture.

2   Combine egg and milk. Pour milk mixture into well in dry ingredients and mix to form a soft dough. Shape dough into a large round, place on an aluminium foil-lined baking tray and cover loosely with aluminium foil.

3   Place baking tray on rack in barbecue and cook for 30 minutes or until damper sounds hollow when tapped on the base.

Serves 6

FESTIVE SMOKED TURKEY

1 cup/125 g/4 oz smoking chips
$^1/_2$ cup/125 mL/4 fl oz brandy
3 kg/6 lb turkey, neck and giblets
removed, trimmed of excess fat
$^1/_2$ cup/125 mL/4 fl oz chicken stock
2 tablespoons vegetable oil

SAGE AND RICE STUFFING
60 g/2 oz butter
1 leek, thinly sliced
4 spring onions chopped
3 rashers bacon, chopped
1 cup/60 g/2 oz breadcrumbs, made
from stale bread
60 g/2 oz pecans, chopped
2 tablespoons chopped fresh sage or
1 teaspoon dried sage
$1^1/_2$ cups/280 g/9 oz rice, cooked

The quantity of smoking chips used will determine the final flavour of the smoked food. For a guide follow the manufacturer's instructions, but don't be afraid to experiment.

Disposable aluminium foil trays available from supermarkets are ideal for putting the smoking chips in.

1   Soak smoking chips in brandy in a non-reactive metal dish for 1 hour.

2   To make stuffing, melt butter in a frying pan over a medium heat, add leek and spring onions and cook, stirring, for 3 minutes. Add bacon and cook for 5 minutes longer. Add breadcrumbs, pecans and sage and cook, stirring, for 5 minutes or until breadcrumbs are crisp. Remove from heat, add rice and mix to combine.

3   Preheat covered barbecue to a medium heat. Place dish, with smoking chips in, in barbecue over hot coals, cover barbecue with lid and heat for 5-10 minutes or until liquid is hot.

4   Spoon stuffing into body cavity of turkey. Secure openings with metal or bamboo skewers. Tuck wings under body and tie legs together. Place turkey on a wire rack set in a roasting tin. Combine stock and oil and brush over turkey.

5   Position roasting tin containing turkey on rack in barbecue, cover barbecue with lid and smoke, basting frequently, for $2^1/_2$-3 hours or until turkey is cooked.

Serves 8

UNDERCOVER CHICKEN

1.5 kg/3 lb chicken, cleaned
125 g/4 oz butter, softened
1 clove garlic, crushed
2 tablespoons snipped fresh chives
2 tablespoons chopped fresh parsley
1 tablespoon olive oil
8 slices prosciutto or lean ham
1 cup/250 mL/8 fl oz white wine

Do not handle cooked and uncooked meat and poultry at the same time. This encourages the transfer of bacteria from raw food to cooked food. Always make sure that you have a clean tray or dish to place barbecued food on – do not place it on the same dish as was used for holding it raw – unless it has been thoroughly washed in hot soapy water.

1   Preheat covered barbecue to a medium heat. Wash chicken inside and out and pat dry with absorbent kitchen paper.

2   Place butter, garlic, chives and parsley in a bowl and mix to combine.

Using your fingers, loosen skin on breast of chicken. Push butter mixture under skin and smooth out evenly. Place chicken on a wire rack set in a roasting tin and brush with oil. Place prosciutto or ham over chicken breast in a criss-cross pattern and secure in place with wooden toothpicks or cocktail sticks. Pour wine over chicken.

3   Place roasting tin on rack in barbecue, cover barbecue with lid and cook for $1^1/2$ hours or until chicken is tender. Cover and stand for 10 minutes before carving.

Serves 6

INDIVIDUAL ANTIPASTO COBBS

Left: Undercover Chicken
Above: Individual Antipasto Cobbs

2 yellow or red peppers, seeded and cut into quarters
$^1/2$ bunch English spinach
4 rosetta or crusty bread rolls
2 cloves garlic, crushed
$^1/4$ cup/60 mL/2 fl oz olive oil
185 g/6 oz marinated feta cheese, crumbled
90 g/3 oz sun-dried tomatoes
185 g/6 oz marinated artichoke hearts, sliced
125 g/4 oz grated Parmesan cheese

1   Preheat covered barbecue to a high heat. Place yellow or red peppers on rack and cook for 15-20 minutes or until skins are charred and blistered. Place peppers in a plastic food bag or paper bag and set aside until cool enough to handle. Remove skin from peppers and cut into thick strips. Boil, steam or microwave spinach until tender, drain and set aside to cool. Squeeze as much moisture as possible from spinach.

2   Cut a slice from top of rolls and reserve. Using a teaspoon scoop out centre of roll leaving a 1 cm/$^1/2$ in shell.

3   Combine garlic and oil and brush over insides of rolls and cut surfaces of tops. Fill rolls with layers of spinach, feta cheese, yellow or red peppers, sun-dried tomatoes and artichokes. Sprinkle with Parmesan cheese and cover with tops. Wrap rolls in aluminium foil and place on rack in barbecue, cover barbecue with lid and cook for 15 minutes or until cheese melts and rolls are crisp.

Serves 4

Packed with a wonderful selection of vegetables and cheeses these filled and barbecued rolls are an imaginative vegetarian alternative.

67

HONEY-GLAZED SMOKED HAM

Smoking wood is available as either chips, chunks or sawdust. Sawdust burns more quickly than chips and chips burn more quickly than chunks. The quicker the wood burns the hotter the heat produced. If chunks are available they are usually a better choice for longer cooking foods.

To remove skin from ham, cut a scallop pattern through the skin around the shank bone, then, starting at the broad end of the ham and using your fingers, gently ease skin away from the fat.

1 cup/125 g/4 oz smoking chips
3 star anise
1 tablespoon finely grated orange rind
$^1/_2$ cup/125 mL/4 fl oz red wine
3-4 kg/6-8 lb cooked leg ham, skin removed and trimmed of excess fat
$^1/_2$ cup/170 g/5$^1/_2$ oz honey
2 tablespoons Dijon mustard
1 cup/250 mL/8 fl oz pineapple juice
whole cloves

1 Place smoking chips, star anise, orange rind and wine in a non-reactive metal dish and stand for 1 hour.

2 Using a sharp knife score the fat of the ham in a diamond pattern – take care not to cut through into the meat.

3 Preheat covered barbecue to a medium heat. Place dish, with smoking chips in, in barbecue over hot coals, cover barbecue with lid and heat for 5-10 minutes or until liquid is hot.

4 Place honey, mustard and pineapple juice in a saucepan, bring to the boil, then reduce heat and simmer, stirring, for 5 minutes or until mixture thickens slightly. Place ham on a wire rack set in a roasting tin, brush with honey mixture and press a clove into the centre of each diamond.

5 Position roasting tin containing ham on rack in barbecue, cover barbecue with lid and smoke, basting occasionally, for 1$^1/_2$-2 hours or until ham is tender.

Serves 15-20

SMOKED MIXED NUTS

When using wood or wood products for barbecuing or smoking always use untreated wood. Those products specifically sold for barbecuing and smoking will be free of chemicals. Hickory wood is a popular choice for smoking, but there are other woods available which impart different flavours – so experiment and find your favourite.

250 g/8 oz raw almonds
185 g/6 oz macadamia nuts
185 g/6 oz raw peanuts
125 g/4 oz raw hazelnuts
125 g/4 oz raw cashews
2 tablespoons smoking sawdust
1 tablespoon sea salt, crushed

1 Preheat covered barbecue to a medium heat. Place almonds, macadamia nuts, peanuts, hazelnuts and cashews on a baking tray and toss to combine.

2 Place sawdust in a metal dish and place in barbecue over hot coals.

3 Position baking tray containing nuts on rack in barbecue, cover barbecue with lid and smoke for 30 minutes. Remove nuts from heat, add salt and toss to coat. Serve hot, warm or cold.

Serves 4-6

Honey-glazed Smoked Ham, Smoked Mixed Nuts

WARM POTATO SALAD

1 kg/2 lb baby potatoes
12 baby onions, halved
8 slices prosciutto or lean ham
$^1/4$ cup/60 mL/2 fl oz olive oil
8 sprigs fresh rosemary
1 teaspoon sea salt
4 spring onions, chopped

MINT DRESSING
1 cup/200 g/6$^1/2$ oz low-fat
natural yogurt
3 tablespoons mayonnaise
2 tablespoons wholegrain mustard
2 tablespoons chopped fresh mint

Remember always to check the manufacturer's instructions that come with your barbecue. Not only will this ensure that you are aware of any special safety requirements but it will also make you aware of your barbecue's full potential as an alternative method of cooking.

1   Preheat covered barbecue to a high heat. Bring a saucepan of water to the boil, add potatoes and onions and cook for 5 minutes. Drain well.

2   Place potatoes, onions and prosciutto or ham in a lightly oiled roasting tin, brush vegetables with oil, scatter with rosemary and sprinkle with salt. Place roasting tin on rack in barbecue, cover barbecue with lid and cook, turning vegetables occasionally, for 20 minutes or until potatoes are tender.

3   To make dressing, place yogurt, mayonnaise, mustard and mint in a bowl and mix to combine.

4   Drain oil from potato mixture and place potatoes and onions in a large salad bowl. Break prosciutto or ham into bite-sized pieces. Add prosciutto or ham and spring onions to potato mixture. Spoon over dressing, toss to combine and serve immediately.

Serves 6

ROASTED TOMATO SALAD

12 plum (egg or Italian) tomatoes,
halved
12 cloves garlic, peeled
$^1/4$ cup/60 mL/2 fl oz olive oil
$^1/2$ teaspoon sea salt
freshly ground black pepper
185 g/6 oz yellow teardrop or
cherry tomatoes
1 red onion, thinly sliced
12 fresh basil leaves, shredded
2 tablespoons balsamic vinegar

Heavy duty oven mitts or oven cloths are essential for safe barbecuing.

1   Preheat covered barbecue to a high heat. Place plum (egg or Italian) tomatoes and garlic cloves on a wire rack set in a roasting tin, brush with oil and sprinkle with salt and black pepper to taste.

2   Place roasting tin on rack in barbecue, cover barbecue with lid and cook for 30-40 minutes or until tomatoes are soft and garlic is golden. Set aside to cool slightly.

3   Place roasted tomatoes, garlic, teardrop or cherry tomatoes and red onion in a bowl. Scatter with basil, drizzle with vinegar and toss.

Serves 4

Warm Potato Salad, Roasted Tomato Salad

Blue plates Villeroy & Boch

Above: Mango Berry Pudding
Right: Summer Peaches

MANGO BERRY PUDDING

1 loaf walnut bread, sliced
2 mangoes, stoned, peeled and sliced
250 g/8 oz blueberries
250 g/8 oz raspberries
$^1/_2$ cup/90 g/3 oz brown sugar
2 cups/500 mL/16 fl oz cream
(double)
$^1/_2$ cup/125 mL/4 fl oz milk
3 eggs, lightly beaten
1 tablespoon brandy
1 teaspoon vanilla essence

1   Preheat covered barbecue to a medium heat. Line base of a lightly greased ovenproof dish with bread slices. Top with one-quarter of the mangoes, one-quarter of the blueberries and one-quarter of the raspberries, then sprinkle with one-quarter of the brown sugar. Top with a layer of bread and repeat layers, finishing with a layer of bread, to use all ingredients.

2   Combine cream, milk, eggs, brandy, and vanilla essence in a bowl and carefully pour over bread and fruit.

3   Place ovenproof dish on rack in barbecue, cover barbecue with lid and cook for 40 minutes or until pudding is firm.

The walnut bread used in this recipe is available from speciality bread shops. If it is unavailable any nut or fruit bread can be used instead.

Serves 6

72

SUMMER PEACHES

4 large freestone peaches, halved and
stones removed
100 g/3^1/$_2$ oz ricotta cheese
30 g/1 oz hazelnuts, roasted and
chopped
2 tablespoons maple syrup
185 g/6 oz amaretti biscuits, crushed
60 g/2 oz butter melted

1   Preheat covered barbecue to a
high heat. Place peaches in a nonstick
baking dish.

2   Place ricotta cheese, hazelnuts
and maple syrup in a bowl and mix
to combine. Fill cavity of each peach
with ricotta mixture.

3   Place amaretti biscuits and butter in
a bowl, mix to combine and sprinkle
over peaches. Place baking dish on rack
in barbecue, cover barbecue with lid
and cook for 15 minutes or until
peaches are tender.

Serves 4

Any fresh peaches can be
used for this dessert, however
the stones are more easily
and neatly removed from
freestone peaches.

Plate Villeroy & Boch

FINAL TOUCHES

Here you will find a small selection of special, yet easy, salads and desserts to add that final touch to your next barbecue.

RAINBOW SALAD

4 rashers bacon
1 bunch English spinach, leaves
shredded
2 carrots, cut into thin strips
1 yellow pepper, cut into thin strips
1 red pepper, cut into thin strips
125 g/4 oz snow peas (mangetout),
cut into thin strips
185 g/6 oz feta cheese, crumbled
125 g/4 oz walnuts, chopped

CHIVES DRESSING
1 tablespoon snipped fresh chives
$^1/_2$ cup/125 mL/4 fl oz mayonnaise
2 tablespoons tarragon vinegar
freshly ground black pepper

1 Cook bacon under a preheated hot
grill for 5 minutes or until very crisp.
Drain on absorbent kitchen paper and
when cool break into bite-sized pieces.

2 Place spinach, carrots, yellow pepper,
red pepper, snow peas (mangetout)
and bacon in a salad bowl and toss
to combine. Scatter with feta cheese
and walnuts.

3 To make dressing, place chives,
mayonnaise, vinegar and black pepper
to taste in a bowl and whisk to
combine. Drizzle dressing over salad
and serve immediately.

Serves 6

This salad looks great
served on a bed of mixed
lettuce leaves on a large
serving platter.

GREEN SEED SALAD

Oven temperature
180°C, 350°F, Gas 4

3 slices wholemeal bread, crusts
trimmed
1 clove garlic, halved
$^1/_4$ cup/60 mL/2 fl oz olive oil
3 tablespoons sunflower seeds
2 tablespoons pumpkin seeds
2 tablespoons sesame seeds
500 g/1 lb assorted salad leaves
2 avocados, stoned, peeled and sliced
250 g/8 oz cherry tomatoes, halved
250 g/8 oz firm tofu, chopped
2 oranges, segmented

CHILLI SESAME DRESSING
$^1/_4$ cup/60 mL/2 fl oz vegetable oil
2 tablespoons lemon juice
1 tablespoon sweet chilli sauce
1 teaspoon soy sauce
1 teaspoon sesame oil

1 Rub bread with cut side of garlic,
brush both sides lightly with olive oil
and cut into 2 cm/$^3/_4$ in cubes. Place
bread cubes on a nonstick baking tray
and bake for 10 minutes or until bread
is golden and crisp. Cool slightly.

2 Place sunflower, pumpkin and
sesame seeds on a nonstick baking tray
and bake for 3-5 minutes or until
golden. Cool slightly.

3 Place salad leaves, avocados,
tomatoes, tofu and oranges in a salad
bowl and toss. Sprinkle with croûtons
and toasted seeds.

4 To make dressing, place oil, lemon
juice, chilli sauce, soy sauce and sesame
oil in a bowl and whisk to combine.
Drizzle dressing over salad and serve
immediately.

Serves 6

Sunflower, pumpkin and
sesame seeds are available
from health food shops or
the health food section of
larger supermarkets.

Pesto Pasta Salad

PESTO PASTA SALAD

375 g/12 oz pasta of your choice
250 g/8 oz cherry tomatoes
125 g/4 oz snow pea (mangetout)
sprouts or watercress
1 green pepper, chopped
2 tablespoons pine nuts

PESTO DRESSING
1 bunch fresh basil
3 tablespoons pine nuts
3 tablespoons grated Parmesan cheese
1 clove garlic, crushed
$^1/_2$ cup/125 mL/4 fl oz mayonnaise
2 tablespoons water

1   Cook pasta in boiling water in a large saucepan following packet directions. Drain, rinse under cold running water and set aside to cool completely.

2   Place pasta, tomatoes, snow pea (mangetout) sprouts or watercress and green pepper in a salad bowl and toss to combine.

3   To make dressing, place basil leaves, 3 tablespoons pine nuts, Parmesan cheese, garlic, mayonnaise and water in a food processor or blender and process until smooth. Spoon dressing over salad and sprinkle with remaining pine nuts.

Serves 6

This salad looks pretty when made with attractive pasta shapes such as bows, spirals or shells. Choose the pasta to suit the other dishes you are serving, for example, if serving the salad with fish, shells would be the perfect choice.

Plate Villeroy & Boch Bowl Accoutrement

WATERMELON GRANITA

¹/2 cup/125 g/4 oz sugar
²/3 cup/170 mL/5¹/2 fl oz water
750 g/1¹/2 lb watermelon, seeded and
skinned, flesh chopped
1 tablespoon lime juice

For an extra special touch, spoon a tablespoon of strawberry- or raspberry-flavoured liqueur over the granita just before serving.

1 Place sugar and water in a small saucepan over a low heat and cook, stirring constantly, for 4-5 minutes or until sugar dissolves. Bring mixture to the boil, then reduce heat and simmer for 4 minutes. Remove pan from heat and set aside to cool.

2 Place watermelon in a food processor or blender and process until smooth.

3 Stir watermelon purée and lime juice into sugar syrup, pour into a freezerproof container and freeze for 1 hour or until ice crystals start to form around the edge. Using a fork, stir to break up ice crystals. Freeze for 2 hours longer, then stir again. To serve, flake with a fork and pile into dessert glasses.

Serves 6

SUMMER BERRY JELLY

2 cups/500 mL/16 fl oz Lambrusco or
sweet red wine
¹/2 cup/125 mL/4 fl oz water
2 tablespoons caster sugar
1 vanilla bean (pod)
2 tablespoons gelatine
500 g/1 lb mixed berries, such as
strawberries, raspberries, blueberries

1 Place wine, water, sugar and vanilla bean (pod) in a saucepan over a high heat and bring to the boil. Reduce heat to simmering, sprinkle over gelatine and stir to dissolve. Remove pan from heat and set aside to cool until warm. Remove vanilla bean (pod).

2 Arrange berries in a 4 cup/1 litre/1³/4 pt capacity oiled jelly mould. Carefully pour wine mixture over fruit and refrigerate until set.

3 To turn out, dip mould into warm water for a few seconds. Remove from water, dry base of mould, then tip sideways, while at the same time gently pulling the mixture away from the edge of mould. This breaks the air lock. Place a plate over mould and quickly turn both mould and plate upside down and give a sharp shake. The mould should fall onto the plate. If it refuses to move, place a hot, wet cloth over the base of the mould for 10-20 seconds.

Serves 6

Watermelon Granita, Summer Berry Jelly

SWEET POTATO SALAD

315 g/10 oz orange sweet potato, peeled
and cut into 2 cm/³/4 in thick slices
185 g/6 oz white sweet potato, peeled
and cut into 2 cm/³/4 in thick slices
60 g/2 oz butter
2 red onions, finely sliced
1 tablespoon finely grated fresh ginger
1 tablespoon brown sugar
1 tablespoon red wine vinegar
1 cup/200 g/6¹/2 oz low-fat
natural yogurt
3 tablespoons chopped fresh dill

1 Boil, steam or microwave orange
and white sweet potatoes until just
tender. Drain and set aside to cool.

2 Melt butter in a frying pan over a
medium heat, add onions, ginger, sugar
and vinegar and cook, stirring, for
15 minutes or until onions starts to
caramelise. Remove pan from heat and
set aside to cool.

3 Place sweet potatoes, onion
mixture, yogurt and dill in a bowl
and toss to combine.

Serves 4

MIXED LEAF SALAD

Oven temperature
180°C, 350°F, Gas 4

375 g/12 oz assorted salad leaves

BLUE CHEESE CROUTONS
250 g/8 oz soft blue cheese
¹/4 cup/60 g/2 oz sour cream
2 tablespoons chopped fresh parsley
1 small French bread stick, cut into
1 cm/¹/2 in slices

RASPBERRY DRESSING
¹/4 cup/60 mL/2 fl oz raspberry
vinegar
2 tablespoons olive oil
2 teaspoons wholegrain mustard

1 Arrange salad leaves on a serving
platter, cover and chill until required.

2 To make croûtons, place cheese,
sour cream and parsley in a bowl
and mix to combine. Spread cheese
mixture over one side of each bread
slice, place on a baking tray and bake
for 10-15 minutes or until bread is crisp
and golden. Set aside to cool.

3 To make dressing, place vinegar, oil
and mustard in a screwtop jar and
shake well to combine. Just prior to
serving, drizzle dressing over salad and
scatter with croûtons.

Serves 4

Mixes of salad leaves and
herbs are available from
many supermarkets and
greengrocers and make a
great base for salads such
as this one.

INDEX